Mole

Mole

PATRICK WARNER

poems

ANANSI

This edition published in 2009 by
House of Anansi Press Inc.
110 Spadina Avenue, Suite 801
Toronto, ON, M5V 2K4
Tel. 416-363-4343
Fax 416-363-1017
www.anansi.ca

Distributed in Canada by
HarperCollins Canada Ltd.
1995 Markham Road
Scarborough, ON, M1B 5M8
Toll free tel. 1-800-387-0117

Distributed in the United States by
Publishers Group West
1700 Fourth Street
Berkeley, CA 94710
Toll free tel. 1-800-788-3123

House of Anansi Press is committed to protecting our natural environment.
As part of our efforts, this book is printed on paper that contains 100%
post-consumer recycled fibres, is acid-free, and is processed chlorine-free.

13 12 11 10 09   1 2 3 4 5

LIBRARY AND ARCHIVES CANADA CATALOGUING IN PUBLICATION

Warner, Patrick, 1963–
Mole / Patrick Warner.

Poems.
ISBN 978-0-88784-821-6

I. Title.

PS8595.A7756M64 2009   C811'.6   C2008-907525-0

Library of Congress Control Number: 2008941437

Cover design: Bill Douglas at The Bang
Text design and typesetting: Ingrid Paulson

We acknowledge for their financial support of our publishing program
the Canada Council for the Arts, the Ontario Arts Council, and the Government of Canada
through the Book Publishing Industry Development Program (BPIDP).

Printed and bound in Canada

For my mother, with love

Contents

I

The Turn

On a steep hill, in a house for one
with a crooked cat and an antique bell,
in the middle of life. This is the place
where you made the turn, having crossed
the line where you could not tell
real from unreal, the climb from years,
wood from your flesh, fur from desire,
that silver bell from your tongue,
which tells the tale of that lonely time
when you thought you were ill,
thought you could not tell unreal
from real, your years from a hill,
self from a house, lust from a cat,
your talk from the sound of a bell.

Precious

Mouth full of straight pins she looked up over
the ancient horse of the sewing machine;
consonants frayed on her lips as she answered
my questions, part of our rainy day ritual

in which I flipped through the photograph album,
refreshing my snapshot memories of houses
and streets where my mother and father and
sisters and brothers lived before I was born.

I was working my way through the usual list:
which dog was Scutty, which one was Dixie,
when had they lived in Loughrea, when in Dublin,
on what number bus was my father conductor.

I asked and she answered, while outside
rain piddled down on the flat kitchen roof
(that felt roof seamed and beetled with bubbles),
rain flung handfuls of tacks at the window,

that sound drowned out when mother depressed
the leaf-shaped pedal which sat on the floor,
and the second-hand Singer rattled to life,
made my belt buckle nibble the edge of the table.

I was working toward the ritual's high point,
to when I'd remove from the back of the album
white vellum and pulp-flecked miniature envelopes,
each one marked with a name and an age,

each containing a lock of child's hair.
And opening each I would pretend to admire
the snippet of golden hair inside, but really
I only cared about one: mine, clipped at age 2.

Ma, I'd say, looking up, *Ma, is this one mine?*
Mmm, she would say. Or, *Is that not your name?*
her delayed assurances making delicious
that time I existed but could not remember.

Ma! I called out, this time a little bit louder,
is this one mine? Focussed in on her task —
flipping open the spring-loaded trapdoor,
she unscrewed the shiny helmet-like bobbin —

Perhaps! she'd say. Perhaps! Had I misheard,
or was this the sound of a Yes when it's
slurred through a mouth full of pins? And
do I imagine her glass lenses glimmered,

flashed metal, when at last she looked up
and explained to me in her no-nonsense way
that one day one of her darling children—
she couldn't remember which child exactly—

had emptied the envelopes, mixed up the cuttings.
After that, she said, there was no way of telling
whose hair was whose—except for Helen's,
because Helen's hair was always much darker.

Coronation

i.

Never-ending the journey by car, the brute
goodbye, the flight that could not land
at the fog-bound capital, and so by bus
the last two hundred miles from Gander

through a wilderness of white spruce, larch,
white pine, black spruce, tuckamore, birch,
rain zigzagging the lung-sponged glass,
shocks jarring the spine's stack of cups.

Invasive the heat, the dank air, the sound
of accents boxing vowels and consonants,
the disconnects that spawn associations
that strike the mind as questions: why

did my thoughts keep running to Louis XVI—
no answers, but pictures came to mind:
a spry leghorn sprinting around the yard,
under the eyes of sinister country folk,

all of them clearly in on the joke, all waiting
for one to state the profound and obvious,
why this fit and feisty generalissimo,
why this broiler agog with action painting

can't for the life of him understand
what his combed head beneath the block,
what his head with its yellow, grimed beak
opening and closing, is trying to tell him.

ii.

Ten years later, I remembered this trip,
it was April the first as I rounded the corner
to Coronation, and with those few steps
passed by way of a suntrap into summer.

A flock of pigeons pecked among the crystals
where decaying snow banks slithered.
I closed my eyes the better to feel the sun,
to see how it turned my eyelids tangerine.

Hearing a pigeon's rhythmic wood-block coo,
I clapped my hands, felt the whole flock snap
like a hundred fans, as it became airborne,
remaking the world as a great ballroom.

iii.

Such joy, such welcome opened to me
that night I rode the bus to town from Gander:
it was there in the form of Spruce-Up Tailors
who offered me suits of sharp pine needles;

in the form of demure birches turned peelers
of bangles, sleeves, corsets and leggings;
it was in the barren's many-coloured eyes
that squeezed out weak but colourful dyes,

tendered hares to sit on my feet like slippers,
and a spotted lynx to lie and lick on my lap,
while spattered trout trembled and shuddered,
regaled me with tales of salt water.

iv.

It was a dream, I suppose, to wake and see
tall, lit buildings on either side of the parkway
like a city submerged in the horizontal rain,
textured with sleet, snow, ice pellets, hail.

The Interval

Each post struck vibrates with a hum,
blurs outward, become a twin,
before settling back into its shape again.

From a distance I notice a delay
between the hammer strike
and the strike's report.

Scientifically speaking, this
is the time it takes sound to travel.
Whole lives are lived in this interval.

Claremorris

Drop me by dead of night in Dromineen
with a petrol can and a Zippo lighter,
let me find my way through unpeopled places,
hare's-tail sedge to mark my path,
my compass not what the snipe avers,
the best way there is the one unchanged.

I am walking by night to Claremorris,
and something is wrong with my vision
of bar seats melting down chrome legs,
magnums of spirits popping like flares,
pint glasses frosting, bearding.
The best way back is the one unchanged.

I find my way through unpeopled places
now the roads are all blocked
and the obstacles mortgaged by strangers,
or the roads don't go where they once went,
or new roads bypass the town altogether.
The best way back is the one less changed.

Scuts of bog cotton mark my approach
through boot-sucking mud, through snares
of heather, through drains that hold
no reflection, through bramble and briar,
through sheep-wooled barbed wire.
I find my way through unpeopled places.

I am on my way home to confirm,
to raise a long ladder up to the sky,
to pick a way through roof slate and rafter
into an attic space wattled with webs
and littered with glittering fly wings.
I find my way through unpeopled places

in search of a box of old school books.
And it's not the books I'm interested in
but whatever I wrote in their margins.
Now something is wrong with my vision.
I see this as soon as I enter the garden.
The best way back is the one less changed,

over oxidized bed frames, bed springs,
past a greyed mound of grass
that hoards the heat like a crotch,
over ground that is matted with creepers,
with rills underfoot that feel like rough metre.
He was the one said no looking back.

Don't waste your time looking into that mirror.
He was the one said don't raise the ladder
to find in the eavestrough a scaltán,
a Jew's harp with skin, among brooches
of waterlogged moss, hunter green,
patina of pistils to sharpen the focus.

Picket

Five one-gallon cans filled to the brim
with stain, a Doberman Pinscher brown.

Long-handled scraper with cupboard-door grip,
its buttoned-down blade like a hieroglyph.

Four-inch stain brush with bristles that fan
like recently barbered hair on the palm.

Hammer and nails to tap in loose pickets.
Sledge and shims to wedge posts in pockets.

In all, two hundred and forty of them
await a scrape and a new coat of stain.

I begin with rote, with repetitive motion,
work each plank with steady down-strokes,

until self like a muscle absorbed in the task
lifts out of the furrow of nine-to-five angst,

thrills to the scraper, a fearsome machete,
forearms dappled with paint chip confetti,

a ticker tape swirl for this conquering hero
who flays the wood to whiskers and fibre.

But by picket one-twenty or one-twenty-one
I feel the weight of what I've taken on.

Lift comes again when the prep is done.
The stain brush loaded nuzzles the grain

which grizzled and parched drinks it in,
and it's all slap and tickle, all nudge and wink,

as always your cover is what you reveal
(in the end you are what you fully conceal).

Against these slippery notions of artifice
I lever the thought of simple self-sacrifice:

now a queen and a princess saunter on in
tapping packet seeds like tambourines.

As a bubble jet's ink requires the page
the domestic life requires this stage.

But stooping to scrape a picket I missed
I hear only a cold streptococcal lisp.

I'm an actor on stage, act three still to go,
where once was technique I now see only flaw,

to finish the last two sections of fence
feels to the body like an act of violence.

And then—all at once—the work is done.
I look back, but without satisfaction,

and will feel none until a fresh zip of energy
pushes that labour deep into memory,

where it will live as an excised tumour,
with that fence as reminder, a fading suture.

The Archives of Minneapolis

The trail gone cold. The windy streets
of an old Near Eastern town
once buried in ash, once excavated,
once a splash in *Life* and *Time*,
now fill with dust; his search for place,
has led him here today, to this,
the Archives of Minneapolis
to sift through cardboard boxes,
through slivered bricks of acetate,
seed trays bearing mixed bouquets
of virus, fungi, mould and yeast,
to find these flowers eating text,
to sigh and sift some more, to sit
until his hip bone sockets blaze,
until he learns to love the sourness,
the stool-like, bitter leaf-stink taste
that's not quite yet a thought
he passes thumb to tongue.

Psychoacoustics

I slip my arms into my crisp lab-coat.
The years are quietly falling layers
while hours, seconds, and minutes snap
like a flicked ear against the air.

The plug of wax I reamed will make a seal,
bearing the horseshoe shape of my nail,
grow hard as finger and thumb make the O
of divas holding the goose of high C.

Then, whip of corduroy, or my childhood
barber who cut my hair in a bowl shape,
whose squeaky, B-flick, black-bat scissors
jammed with his airy tuneless whistle.

Finger shifts — fine arcs and parentheses fall
like gross snowflakes on linoleum.
I would do anything to shed I, or at least
I who thinks of himself as capital P.

Wax hits the sullied breast-plate or
crest of the fire-grate. The roast-pan
stacked in the dish-rack, cooling,
slips a wanton hip.

Therefore: a theory of sonnets

Therefore, if you want to write in the sonnet form,
it's good to understand the concept of therefore.
                    (Handbook of Poetic Forms, p. 191)

i   The Land Before Time

The land gets bigger from time to time.
Time gets bigger but doesn't get more.
A white notched peg holds down
the billowing marquee of everything
that came before. Us. Animal calls —
the woolly mammoth's fleshy screech,
the great black bear's existential moan.
Our own harpings, hootings, hawkings
announce the dawn.
The spanked bottom of the horizon.
How badly we treat our brothers, make
them wear dresses, ride bicycles,
taunt them with an alphabet. Chimps
cradle jaws and roll their eyes to heaven.

ii Closed Circuit

Mike and Con and his girl Andrea
bumble around in their own little world,
still ruled by Santy, some say Santa,
some see Nicholas in his red and white.
Con comes on like a pro, tells Mike.
Tells how, how not to pull a teen—
Stay out of sight of the guy with the lip,
the short-legged limp.
They speed around on in-line skates,
fuelled by cider and amphetamines,
in the roller rink beside the track,
beside the roundabout that feeds the motorway,
that feeds the whole five ring circus,
throbbing like really massive bass.

iii Mighty Whites

A man (is it me?) in the laundromat
shakes out his teal blue sheets
and curses, God damn you to hell, Dante,
for leaving a tissue up your sleeve.
Moses came down with the mist, you see,
full of whispers, wheezes, and rheum,
gurgling like a cheap coffee machine
in which his followers heard thunder.
Oh, for a mist without aroma,
the companionship of silence,
the gentle foothills of a notion
where we can graze
in the inconclusiveness of togetherness,
where never a clarity can intervene.

Evidence: there will be no evidence

A white film. Some tract turns
to KY-jelly in a can. Overnight,
while you slept, the cat prowled.
Haw, haw says the Michelin man
when the widow cannot pay
her rent. Mt. Fuji quakes;
the straw huts tremble.
The widow's soul is a frail origami,
a parasol that pops open
whenever it rains. Homemade
chips dumped in a deep fat
fryer. The widow nibbles
on an ear of corn while
Mt. Fuji pushes one finger
through the tympanic
taut white seal and into
peanut butter. Evidence:
there will be no evidence.

Except the sides of the bath.
Glistening skin.
Four-leaf clovers on the counter.
Sumotori.
A letter of intent.
Tea stains on the carpet.
A lightweight fedora.
Brittle cocktail decorations.
Brown clouds on the ceiling.
Freckles on Formica.
A string of rosary beads.
The sound of locusts.
A magazine index.
The ABC's of signing.
The fridge door.
Peanut butter
without a hole in it.

Couch Potato

The couch potato gets the cosmic fits
when purple feelers rise up from his pits.
"Feelers, feelings, Ha! Ha! Ha!" he quips.

His will for a long time an axe blade,
but then, one day, the way would not open,
each blow dinged atonally on the grain.

His mood for a longer time a bludgeon,
with a clump of hair stuck off on one side,
like a hair of the dog killed yesterday.

And now these purple feelers rising,
unfolding green serrations on their way
to eat through dental moulding, plaster,

to bracelet whiskery joist and rafter.
The couch potato jerks with laughter.

Entertainment

I was on my way to see a film, *Bewitched*,
to bask in the alien beauty of Nicole Kidman—
I've been obsessed since *Eyes Wide Shut*,
since *Moulin Rouge*, since *Dead Calm*.

It was 3 o'clock on a Saturday afternoon,
and I was not alone. Many hundreds milled
and many hundred more formed lines
that snaked from concessions on either side.

Behind the counters, pock-faced teens
in visors and tight polyester shirts hustled
to fill jumbo popcorns and jumbo drinks,
to fill trays of nachos drenched with cheese.

The line I was in was like a sleeve of cups.
I was like an empty white cardboard cup,
my mood as light as that funnel container
I would soon fill with effervescent desire.

My mind was a cow about to buck and run,
as if to escape some burrowing tick.
My thoughts like spires of rattling grass bent low
that spring back hard scattering seed.

Nothing happened then for the longest time.
The closer I got to the point of service,
the more I dithered between Reese's Pieces
and a giant popcorn with golden topping.

Until—ode to the big bang—out from one end
of that grass seed whiskered a blue white root,
while from the other end uncoiled the palest stalk,
sending forth its green two-blade propeller.

The sun shines. The wind blows. Rain falls.
And everything goes according to plan
until again that hidebound ruminant ark
of complacency comes, this time to graze.

So it is, I thought, the grass blade grows
through meat to make meat and dung
and the musical tympani of milk hitting
the galvanized bucket's freckled bottom.

Salted and churned cream will make butter,
rich living relative of this ghostly topping
that spurts from the stainless steel spigot
known to concession jerks as the jizzer.

The New Economy

I walked to work only to find it closed.
A sign said the workweek was changed
and might change again without notice.
It was a Tuesday, the new weekend.

On the way home there were catcalls.
At my house I found my wife unshaven,
wearing a three-piece suit with wide lapels.
She handed me a gown, said put it on.

That night, in despair, at my friend's place,
I prayed again to the one true God,
and He answered me thus: with the taste
of wheat in my doughy white bread.

The Snows

Snow in summer and snow on the mountain,
snow berry, milkweed, and dandelion seeds
all might have been read as foreshadowing
this glare, this mid-winter snowblink
which renders my neighbour's dog a snow bear,
my neighbour who is from the snow belt
and who for years was the only man
on our block with a snow blower.

Prescient now seem his snow plans
in this winter of 10x snowfall.
A giant, sixty feet tall he reaches
and fills his arms with billowing snow,
snow like sugar hardened from damp,
snow that is like the fine ashes of summer foliage,
snow that groans under boots like boards,
snow that squeaks like a barman's towel,
snow like a horse eating whole pears,
all these he gathers up
and fashions loosely into a bale
he underarms up the garden
where it explodes
into rock fall and powder.

As a man, some find him snow cold,
while his wife (slightly crushed) is a snow queen,
a cone tinted with sweet red syrup.
Dealing with her is a snow-course
where at first one walks with the stiff
splinted legs of the snow crab,
but soon there develops a snow craft,
a feint and thrust to her snow creep,
her devil, and snow drift.

It's a kind of addiction this banter—
my nostrils bell for my snow queen.
I have become a snow dropper,
snow dropping at will from her washing line
her snow white panties, for which
I've become a snow finch, a flea,
a snow fleck, a fly, a snow gnat,
a snow goose for her snow grain and grass,
a snow grouse for her snow gum and snow hole,
a snow leopard crossing the snow line and snow pack
for snow lily, snow pea,
a great snowy owl, a snow petrel, a snow wolf
prowling the snow slip,
hunting the snowmelt for snow mice,
juncos, snow vole and partridge.

Augur

The road was a length of blood-dark gut
stretched on an off-white marble counter.
On the other side, a car flashed lights,
honked and slammed on brakes, slid
to a halt on its duck's black feet.

I watched the driver's side window
descend, a sheet of ice-storm glitter
in time-lapse photography melting,
the old lady driver nodding in time,
a leathery chick pecking through shell.

Some chick, some egg, some place,
I thought, just as she verbed me:
Is it going to storm? she asked. My
mind saw pixels; somewhere in there
was a weather-bomb's sleety vortex.

I'm sorry, I said, but I didn't catch the
forecast. Her features fused.
Can't you tell by the sky?
I cocked my head and looked up,
cast iron pot lid, salt-flecked. Silent.

She spat from the root of language,
horked up a word not yet a word, her
mot juste for disgust. I was chuffed,
buff-happy as a plastic toy placed
with love under a synthetic tree.

This was the gift beyond my meagre
means, the one I wanted so much
I pretended I didn't want it.
It was enough
she saw me as a local man.

She hauled away, her red tail-lights
glowing like Export-A tips flicked
into the mid-Atlantic. I was back in,
alone inside the labyrinth
of ever more complex exclusions,

beginning and ending with
that porthole view on the self,
claimed as objective, third-party,
dispassionate, removed. She had put
her finger on a numb spot—

like a scar in thinking—that all day
had made me irritable, a dread
I now know to be coeval
with atmospheric pressure, and
imminent arrival of new weather.

The Mole

As though a hand had reached inside to rub
my liver. This was the nose of the mole.

Later, I felt a prickle, a draught in my eye.
This was the southwest breeze blowing
where the stone-blind mole had passed.

This was the meat of what was unspoken.
The absolute bedrock of morals, the top-soil
of incomprehension in which you turned
and said: Your wife tells me everything.

This was the unknown known, the mole
surfacing through the green. And blinking
by the swings on that suburban lawn
was my penchant for darkness and filth,
my penchant for sticking my nose in.

The Scientist

Where did the seal heads come from?
They were a present from a fisherman
who wished to woo the scientist.
Not an answer. A queer posy these,
a devalued currency, almost contraband.

Queer to the fisherman her request,
when he would have taken her to a dance,
or out in boat to the island of turrs,
placed her there among the puffy chicks,
her eyes hard and cold as a gull.

And calculating now on the beach
her stance, how to accept this gift from him,
how to turn gift into transaction.
Tie them with rope in a nylon sack,
a nylon rope — chain might be better.

Make do. One makes do in the field.
She looks back at the cone of coiled rope.
Looks for snags. Feels the heft
of the bag as she starts to swing,
rhymes to it with a rock of her hips.

Thinks metronome and swinging scrotum,
then laughs as she tosses it high,
watches its weird centrifuge as it falls,
its Hockneyesque splash,
the rope feed, slacken and curl.

Everything up until now has been
a rehearsal. Time now for action,
for the crab to cock a beady eye,
tilt its way across the sea floor,
time for sea slug, for conner, for lobster,

for starfish, sculpin, and jiggling tides.
In theory, three months' work by these
will strip the harbour seal heads,
leave three seal skulls fresh from the sea,
cold and clean enough to lick.

But in practice, flesh clings stubbornly
and must be picked away with a scalpel,
a job the scientist will delegate,
not wanting to relinquish objectivity.
So in latex gloves, with blade and hook

the student help sets out to unsculpt
actual flesh from actual seal. In cotton
masks they face their subjects, their eyes
dark and water-filled as they inhale
the sea's brine and onion smell.

The Pews

If that hardwood spoke redemption,
it was a message coded in the form,
in how the pew backs rolled vertebrae
that was part massage, part rosary.

And if that hardwood spoke for the weak,
it was the gun stock I felt when I laid
my cheek a certain way and sighted,
down the line, a kneeling enemy.

And if that hardwood spoke of elevation,
it was in the cursive free-hand grain,
and in the peppery raw-wood smell
that oils and varnish could not conceal,

that coaxed my nostril's shy snail foot
to creep along the pew-back's rail,
until its wax and spice ignited sneezes,
great earth-shaking bugle blasts

that cleared the way for other scents:
soaps and Right Guard antiperspirant,
tidal waves of Old Spice aftershave,
hairsprays that hacked bronchial tubes,

mints melting on the heights of halitosis,
lavender tucked into beds of cold cream,
and above it all, the whiskey-like whiff
and heavy musk of expensive perfumes.

Whenever I think of hardwood pews
I think of these olfactory disguises
that sanctified but could not hide the news
from the most angelic of our senses.

Snowbirds

Though I struggle, it won't be with moral choices;
an overnight flight from winter to summer
may result in wrongfooting the senses,
as sticking your hand under a running tap
and being unable to say if it's cold or hot

starts a six-day-all-inclusive package junket,
a six-day-all-you-can-eat-and-drink excursion,
with full limousine service from the airport
to this hotel resort. Hardly enough time
to acclimatize—but somehow I'll enjoy it!

Enjoy the view through these sunglasses
with palm-trunk arms and fronds over frames,
bought from a crippled vendor named Juan
someone—he either said "Juan" or "I am,"
whatever! I had to buy to get rid of him.

As if I hadn't contributed enough
to the local economy—but forget about him
and his tin shack town just over the hill,
enjoy how these lenses turn the ocean red
and the surf, where it breaks, to pink lace.

I will enjoy the form of the American surfer,
by his crewcut hair, I'll guess, a military advisor,
cock-of-the-walk as he rides a rolling comber,
and forget what I've read about local police
and their unofficial war against the homeless.

I will enjoy the beautiful girls on the beach,
all locals, and not one afraid of being topless,
especially this one who sticks out her tongue
when she catches me watching her watching him,
that surfer turtling seaward through the swell.

She will torment for the rest of the week,
reminding me of what it was like to be young,
and without inhibition. I will think of her
as I flip-flop my way through the tide pools,
gathering whelks, mussels and sea snails

And I'll recall, over papaya, the newspaper piece
(Focus section from the *Globe*, weekend edition)
about workers on these exclusive resorts,
and how the radiant eyes of young women
do not signify natural health but malnutrition.

Which will make it harder to live vicariously
through this surfer, to enjoy his reach,
as he makes one more run from the sea
to where they wait on the rose-tinted beach.
This is how it will go for the rest of the week:

I will sit at the piss-warmed swim-up bar.
I will read a novel each day before lunch.
I will graze the buffet in my flowery shirt.
I will sit in my chair sipping tropical punch,
not quite settling; in fact, with days still to go

I will notice how things have started to smell,
like that forgotten bucket left out by the door,
that one as a child I would carefully fill
with starfish, sand dollars, crab shells,
an assortment of poignant seaside mementos.

Starlings

In a nearby maple,
spanworms gnaw
leaves to their girders.

When the sun shines
they'll rappel
down long silk threads,
like Special Forces.

And the starling,
he's no machine gun,
he'll run out of bullets
before he can finish them.

Waxwings

Months of winter weather
like hard labour
and tomorrow the same
all over again.

What do I care if waxwings
swoop to flense
the last few berries
from the dogberry tree?

They put me in mind
of my well-heeled friends
with their flowery shirts,
their pharmaceutical tans.

The Hinge

Sometime after the steady breathing,
like someone slowly sweeping a yard,
but sometime before the beetling eyeballs,
you move that squeaky hinge in your throat.
This is the sound of the door swinging open
and shut as you pass into sleep.
This is the sound of your going away.

I've heard myself make the same sound
while listening as if from underground.
And I have been known to make it as well
when I remember something painful.
This is the sound of the door swinging shut
as I heave my body against it.
This is the sound of keeping-at-bay.

The Lost Years

i.

Rip the flex from the electric clock,
braid bare wire ends to the steel sieve's rim,
and plop it like a helmet on your skull.
Now reach and plug the three-pin in.

The shyest creatures come out to play:
wild lynx, mink and whiskered otter;
wrist-thick trout that tremble and shudder,
regale you with tales of salt water.

Now write of your fabled breakthrough,
the wall cracking open below the clock,
no Narnia fur-trimmed portal this,
but the broken teeth of chiselled brick,

with the frayed ends of one-inch slats
and fat-lip lumps of mortar hanging loose.
Earphones like moss pads over ears
with *Back in Black* on continuous loop,

that demolition soundtrack giving way
to something altogether country:
birdsong, and nearby a trickling brook,
sunlight filtering down through a canopy,

and awe like a shock of long thick hair:
like that aforementioned colander
hot-wired to frig the hard-wired brain,
and shock you into the free-and-clear,

so real, at three A.M., when every beer,
when every tumbler of amber rum,
lighting the way from there to here,
shone like a lantern, frail and paper-thin.

ii.

The sun that day was not the sun I knew.
Crash-test dummy amperes struck on anvil ohms
unzipping phosphorescent candles, hot-car joules.

So cruel the way its gammas sparked gamin,
the way it powered down, obliterating shade,
green-housing me, by a no-name petrol station.

Later, the fumy pumps were lanced, the tuberous
tanks dug up, the toy-land car-port canopy knocked
and carted off. The shop converted to a key & lock.

Tulk's, a name I often think of when I think about
the interval between that pot-bound, heat-struck day,
and the day I surfaced, a hemisphere away,

sockless, shoeless, shirtless, clueless, with nothing
but a pair of check pants bunching up my balls
and the memory of wind whipping past my ears,

a bellows that fanned the embers of that sun
with everything pent up, jammed, stuck, on hold
about to rip through muscle, burst through skin.

iii.

Ashen my younger face emerging
from the ashtray's mush of ash stabbed
with burned-out Seadogs, jack-knifed butts.

Dusty footsteps lead across the floor
between black moons of long-playing albums,
lead all the way to the double bay

that overlooks the hard-tramped snow,
the aftermath of what? a lover's dance,
a midnight stagger around a streetlamp,

hands warming in each other's pants,
footsteps frozen at twenty below.
We were young. Then came the thaw.

Like jump-leads, these butter knives,
their blackened tips still surface
in our kitchen drawer from time to time.

Historical

We barbered roots with trowels.
Heard in singing steel alarm.
In each opened canvas square
buried bricks made Braques.
Scoured shade for artefacts.

Dug trenches six-feet deep.
Chucked up bricks and rocks.
Bagged cloudy window pane.
Bagged rust-furred cut nails.
Bagged tin-glazed stoneware.

Took pleasure in the lore:
Punty marks on bottle bases.
Bubbles proved hand-blown glass.
Bore widths dated pipe stems.
Porous clay ware stuck to lips.

Disbelieved the archaeologist
Who said it was a hospital.
It was all one hurried backfill.
Laboured through a schism.
Acquired air of professionalism.

Found the find of the summer:
Found wrist-thick and warm.
Found swear-to-God-it-had-a-pulse.
Found rope-like-root-like thing.
Found dinged when it was hit

And where dinged winked silver,
Like lead before it darkens.
Found strong enough to stand on.
Found the main power supply
Nowhere near where it should be.

Enough juice, said the engineer,
A Scot from the Hebrides,
To melt your hands and feet,
Turn your hair to a corona of flame,
Send you home in a zip-lock baggie.

Sermon to the Immigrants

I tell them to embrace their confusion,
let the conceits of culture and place
fall away to reveal a true, new face,
a face that will last only one generation.

But they only mutter under their breath,
trade jokes about my muddled accent,
married as they are to dénouement,
married to the old idea until death.

The Memory Warehouse

Who drops these pallets stacked with boxes
on my wharf? I burp a dry dusty burp,
and my cataract glass rattles,
my shard teeth zing in putty pyorrhoea,
while my clear panes shimmer, show
dock-side bollards dripping guano,
tug-boat and tiny tanker where horizon
bends like re-bar over Punta Cana.

> Inside, there's nothing much to see.
> It's all a cube van hither and thither.
> Today we are headed to where Aisle 7
> memories were originally gathered
> (as is the case with memories,
> these memories are encased in ice).
> WARNING: the cube van's chiller's broken,
> what comes back may be distorted!

And the drivers—Eeech!—the drivers,
old axe-faced, phlegmy Mr. Hunger,
and young Master Poverty-of-the-Moment—
sometimes the latter brings himself back.
I should say the atmosphere inside
the drivers' lounge is gloomy: bottles
under benches, Vesuvius ashtrays,
occasional lapses into Movement poetry.

Meanwhile, out back behind the concrete wall

    (my back's unplastered,
    the cement between the blocks hardened
    where block weight sloshed it,
    the whole retaining force aerosoled
    with colourful half-truths, the ground
    littered with the detritus of mind blowing:
    petal shards strewn, punctured
    cans, archipelagos of cigarette butts,
    a rogue turd expelled when
    some solvent shined a gut)

on the other side, past the partitioned
highway and over another wall,
is a neighbourhood much like the one
where it all began, where nothing much
has changed, where no one has died,
where the neighbours all look the same,
just older, where they remember you,
talk to you as if you'd just been away
a few days, where even the town
after the recent unbelievable
building boom looks much the same,
the bones still visible under tightly
stretched streets and botoxed greens.

IV

The Poet

I might say a train stopped
then started up again

I might say the engine cut
as we hurtled, express,
from resort town to metropolis

I might say the engine cut
and the train drifted
sighed, was the idle heart
at the middle of nowhere

I might say greenness
surrounded us there
and that a country silence
crept in, began to graze
on our vowels and consonants

until there came a thump
as though some outer door had shut
in the green middle of nowhere
and the engine lurched ahead
resumed its glide to speed
past banks of rhododendron

where the engine had suddenly
stopped and silence crept in
and along with silence came this boy
a family had brought to set aboard
I might call him their first born
now striding up the passageway
and searching every stranger's
face for signs of welcome

I might say we seemed no match
for him, even as the engine ate
the silence in the green
middle of no place, where
gathering speed we slid
toward the great metropolis
while a boy searching for a seat
searched every stranger's face
for something hidden

and I would be remiss not to say
that we kept up our indifference
our coolness to his gaze
that offered to return to us
something we had misplaced
in the great grey metropolis
and had thought to find again
in a lakeside resort town
on the edge of nowhere
at the grey green end of the line

though secretly we wondered
if we ever had possessed
whatever it was his steady gaze
promised to replace in us
something of that silent green
that grazed upon us when
the engine cut and the train
sighed, slowed, stopped
in the middle of nowhere
where a boy walked toward us
as his family walked away

The Touch Tank

The journeyman-welded crabs move stiffly
around inside the armour of their PhD's,
and with buck-stop stares contemplate attack.
Delicate flywheel motions near their mouths
suggest the nuanced exploration of this
thought: sideways-forward or sideways back.

Nearby, artistic whelks confect ice-cream
dollop shells through which project soft
white sprouts of feeling, and extrude, below
their skeletons of fine Spode china, skirts of
same white flesh, houndstooth-flecked;
underneath, you know, they're all vagina.

A lead-foot shellfish revs, propels its bulk
along the bottom—its square hinge denotes
a scallop not a clam. Look! says someone,
pointing to an orange marble with a turban.
That, says the interpreter, is a sea peach,
and immediately ten little hands all reach.

Nearby, a pinkish bombed-out minaret
makes to the ear an age-old invitation,
until a hermit crab extends a clutch of claws.
Above, tumescent, slimy, warty and green,
a hoisted sea cucumber deftly shucks its
dildo status by pissing gently in the stream.

Who knew the inner life was this small
aquatic town, where a slightly wavering
whitish outline around everything suggests
a time before our principles took hold,
before the whore's egg spawned a crown,
before a maimed starfish jigged cruciform.

Basho

So this is where the lawyers go for lunch
and the arts administrator and the gallery
director soon to blow town. Rumour has it
that as haute couture is to off-the-rail
so Basho is to lunchtime fare. This is where
the poets come to celebrate and spend
their share of the public purse, a recent win.

One feels obliged to comment on the décor.
Did I mention the table's angled edges
that suggest, from overhead, the rhombus.
There's a salt water aquarium with living rock,
not coral — that would probably be illegal.
We could ask the lawyers, her, in pinstripe,
or him, contemplating a second run for office.

One feels obliged to remark on the food.
The poets consult the menu and order
nigiri, ten. One rice bowl. And Oh, two miso.
The muddy miso soup recalls the rice field
and the green onion swirl a magic 8 ball.
She likes it, but he does not, except for
the post-coital or oyster-like aftertaste.

Me so horny, he thinks to say, except
he fears that she might take him up on it.
Remember that scene in *Full Metal Jacket*,
the skinny hooker arrives on a motorbike
but will not service the African American —
he registers Sapporo's pint-tin jujitsu,
decides to stick to the form, which is gossip.

A fin of wasabi breaches the surface of each plate.
Mix it in with the dish of soy, she says.
The soy sauce like fine sewing-machine oil
does nothing to mellow the mint-green wasabi
which will ride his oesophagus hard for
the next twenty-four hours. Horseradish,
the active ingredient, horseradish and fish.

Nigiri ten is a platter of ten different sushi.
His favourite's a rice ball wrapped in tuna —
stretched labia majora lit from the inside.
And as well he likes the saddling eel slice,
surely a foreskin pan-fried to a crisp?
There is also a delicate seaweed collar
topped with roe that's the colour of amber.

And speaking of roe, the rice bowl glitters
with tiny ruby-red eggs that pop like stitches
when bitten. From the aquarium, a whiskery
red and white racing-car shrimp watches,
and a Jagger-lipped fish who half-swims
and half-lurches around on sleeve-like fins.
Both of the poets fall in love with him.

The Children of Critics

1.

The children of critics exist as a hunger.
On stick-like legs with bulbous joints they tap
Morse code on pressure-treated lumber,

usually at dusk, in that time between
a quarter to eight and eight-fifteen,
in September, when the wind smells of tea,

when the moon's a CD, when with a quiver
it pulls the inside out and the outside in
until neck hairs parse an authentic shiver.

2.

The children of critics delight in connection.
In the future, the father's once sickly son
will hunger for all things Southeast Asian,

his imagination long since inflected
by a photo that smelled of pepper wood
that was planted inside the cover of a book

entitled *Lost Flora of Indonesia*—
an invitation from his shadow brother
whose ambrosial presence posits amnesia.

Reading

Some say it looks like a siphoning hose
while others say that it's more like a stem;
some say it unfurls up from the spine,
and a few that it periscopes out from
the page. Still more contend this is all wrong,
that it happens the other way round:
it begins as a nub between the eyes
and then sprouts like an antler or horn.

Some say mineral, some vegetable,
still others hold its kingdom is animal —
among these are a few who will point
to the garden slug's mating ritual,
particularly to spotted leopards or greys
who, suspended on bungees of slime,
produce from the shoulder sex organs
which change as they slowly entwine.

Some say to watch is to be a voyeur
and that watching is somehow perverted,
and yet these few of religious upbringing
seem disposed to being converted:
news of a visible swirl in the siphon
and they are quickly up on the stump,
describing the swirl as sleet in the snot-
coloured bulb at the side of a gas pump.

Though whether this fluttering movement
is one way only—from book into brain—
or is somehow the other way round
is the subject of heated protracted debate:
does it pull like a plant up from the soil;
and is it capable of changing course;
or does it trick the eye the way a turning wheel
on slowing seems to run in reverse?

Among these a critical few will venture
(with barely concealed abhorrence)
that the change for both reader and book
is a movement away from presence.
Others, seized by this point, will say
the only real change comes later,
when the reader, flushed, snaps shut
the book, leaves off this lightest of labours

and splay-limbed languorously stretches,
so that hair roots retract into the spine
and begonias or hardy lupines bloom
where a rush of blood pools in the groin;
proof positive, surely, of appetite whetted,
of the trying on of a new perspective
in which ordinary everyday things
are found somehow less expected.

Bibby Wonder

All his days were dirty greys he folded
into tri-point flares, semaphores secured
with the ankle snap of an argyle sock.

Only one thing whet his ooze to trickle,
made him stare in bibby wonder,
a hutch he filled with fired figurines.

Who saw these figurines as figurative
looked hard at him and tried to guess,
some faulted him, some fell into largesse.

The Old Neighbourhood

It was never great, even back in the day.
Here Kumquat May had her episode:

Jack Hughes! Jack Hughes! she wailed
at a white-haired man, *Der Weiße Engel!*

whose eyes behind tinted lenses flicked
like an analog needle. Then he was gone.

Some say she was his other woman.
Some say her beef was with Guinness

(that black door marked with a toucan)
more than it was with him or his missus,

camogie queen and once runner-up
at the Rose of Tralee: Hurly Mary,

now best known as the mother of Gord,
that poet's poet of the common man,

whose particular brand of strum and dang
can still be heard, from time to time,

the famous twang of that broken string
on *There's a Love Knot in my Laureate*.

But things are better today. Much better!
Streets that once burned like phosphorus

are now prosperous. Signs everywhere:
Spa Wholesaler: Martin Loofah King.

Joomange: French, all kosher, safari.
Prosperous maybe, but still a bit shady:

note the camel-coat crewcuts in suits,
flipping through on-sale racks of thobes,

while a diva in burka winks knowingly
at a man sipping tea in *Mahatma Grande's*.

"Golan shites," the lot of them, says *Lloyd
E. Dawe*, the oldest retailer on the block.

But the old have a way of forgetting
just how bad it was back in the day

with the brothers Quixote, Don and Wiley,
two hard men — no soft centaurs these —

running a little behind from the *Deli Llama*,
selling it to all in tents and porpoises,

but strictly medicinal, the whole front
innocent as chasing rabbits with a hoe.

Innocence thrives where we begin.
My old self follows me around like an

idiot suivant, who knows only one thing
in this world. And how that thing ran true,

and still runs true today. A radical naiveté—
Oh little turd who made thee? Take this

couple, twenty-somethings turned thirty,
who have traded in their designer dogs

for an all-terrain stroller. Hi, Digger!
Hi, Digger, squawks their two-year-old

at an idling truck, a cement mixer,
while twirling a bead with chubby fingers.

His parents gape at him in astonishment.
And I gape in astonishment as well,

when behind them, exiting *The Gap*,
a dwarf in a three-piece pinstripe *Armani*

barks, like some kind of small arms dealer,
into the beak of a throwaway phone.

Premature

Like a tiny toy horse I trolled in the sea,
a black and white horse near the end of my line,
I trolled to see what might be hooked
and though I caught none of the deep sea dark
a lot of strange creatures swam by and looked.

There was Randolph Scott with his thin turkey neck,
nervous and sweating outside the church door,
two hitching posts up from Miss Daisy's Saloon
where the louvered doors swung to and fro,
keeping the beat of what was in store.

It was late Sunday night in front of the telly,
when out of the side of her eye distracting
she kept catching the tap of his green tartan slipper,
the fringe of hair around his scrawny ankle.
Will we go up to bed? she said to my father.

From somewhere high in the air in a corner
I watched her watching him watching her undress
in the dresser mirror. Then she turned, and he
swept back the covers, and they collapsed together,
eight months and two weeks before I was born.

Like a tiny toy horse I trolled in the sea,
a black and white horse near the end of my line,
I trolled to see what might be hooked
and when I was pulled from the deep sea dark
a lot of strange creatures swam by and looked.

Stone

A grey blue stone bifurcated
by a band of sparkling quartz,
glad eye from the Pleistocene,
it sits on my mind's table.
Like sadness, it has the quality
of being wholly passive.
Dark to its core, it glows at dusk
like a dying bulb. Dry but shaped
by water, flung up by streams
and tides it exerts a force
against all expectation.
Seems to be saying anything
may happen: has and will.
One day, you may pick up
that stone and pitch it, leaving
behind a small depression.

Acknowledgements

Thanks to Rochelle for being my first and most graceful reader. And for being beautiful.

Thanks to Annie for the many long walks and conversations about creativity, social relations, and death.

Thanks to Greta for being five and utterly herself: our petal-flower, our pistol.

Thanks to Ken Babstock for his sharp eye and light touch in editing this collection.

Thanks to everyone at House of Anansi Press.

Thanks to Memorial University of Newfoundland, and especially to the staff of the Queen Elizabeth II Library for creating such excellent collections of books and periodicals.

Thanks also to the editors of the following publications in which a number of these poems first appeared: *TickleAce*, *The Newfoundland Quarterly*, *The Fiddlehead*, *The Malahat Review*, *Arc Poetry Magazine*, *Canadian Notes & Queries*, and *Jailbreaks and Re-Creations: 99 Canadian Sonnets*.

About the Author

In 2007, PATRICK WARNER won the E.J. Pratt Poetry Award for his collection *There, there*. His first collection of poetry, *All Manner of Misunderstanding*, was nominated for the 2002 Atlantic Poetry Prize and for the 2003 Newfoundland and Labrador Book Awards. His work has been published in *TickleAce*, *The Fiddlehead*, *Matrix*, *Signal*, the *Sunday Telegram* (St. John's), *Poetry Ireland Review*, and *Metre* (Ireland). He lives in St. John's, Newfoundland.